Soccer Team Notebook

Soccer Team Notebook

Richard Kent and Amy Edwards

A companion book to

Writing on the Bus: Using Athletic Team Notebooks and Journals to Advance Learning and Performance in Sports

WritingAthletes.com

Dedication:

For José Felipe Ytuarte Nuñez . . . *RK*

In celebration of Title IX, for giving me the opportunity to play and coach this beautiful game . . . *AE*

Acknowledgements:

For contributions to our coaching careers and this book, we thank Bryan Blitz, Graham Brown, Mike Keller, Jim Evans, Rick McGuire, Eileen Narcotta-Welp, Stacy Narcotta-Welp, Gayle Sirois, Sheila Stawinski, Bill Swartz, and Anne Wood.

NATIONAL WRITING PROJECT

This book is published in cooperation with the National Writing Project, University of California, 2105 Bancroft Way, Berkeley, CA 94720

Contents

Introduction..7

Pre- Mid- Post-Season Thoughts......................9

Match Analyses I..27

Match Analyses II...81

Performance Feedback...................................95

Athletic Journals...113

Team-Building Activities..............................179

Injury Rehabilitation Plans..........................191

Note Pages..197

Coach's Comments.......................................221

About the Authors..227

Introduction

"Success is no accident. It is hard work, perseverance, learning, studying, sacrifice and most of all, love of what you are doing or learning to do."
— Pele

For Players

The notebook you have in your hands can help you to become a better soccer player. By completing the book's activities, you will stay more organized and learn more about soccer and about yourself as a player.

This notebook will not replace good coaching or dedicated training. You're not going to instantaneously run faster or score more goals because you wrote a Match Analysis or reflected on your play. But maintaining this notebook will make you a more knowledgeable athlete, and with that knowledge you will improve... and so will your team.

Our best advice about your writing is to remember that this is your notebook. You have to write what is true for you as a soccer player and person. Do your best to stay balanced in your writing. This notebook is a place to learn, grow, and improve... a place to write about yourself as a player and teammate while always imagining your best. We challenge you to think deeply, to explore your understanding of the game, and to see yourself at the next level.

Protect your notebook in a zip-lock plastic bag and keep it in your soccer kit. Carry a spare pen or pencil. You may end up sharing certain pages of your notebook with teammates and the coaching staff, so do your best to write legibly.

Finally, you should know that elite athletes like Olympians analyze their training and competitions in training logs, notebooks, and journals. Why is writing such a powerful way to learn? Author William Zinsser explains,

"Writing organizes and clarifies our thoughts. Writing is how we think our way into a subject and make it our own. Writing enables us to find out what we know—and what we don't know—about whatever we're trying to learn."

Play well. Enjoy your teammates and the *beautiful game.*

For Coaches

As coaches, we never stop looking for ways to guide our players and teams to the next level. This book can complement your coaching practice, but only you can determine how.

Sport psychologists assign writing to help athletes look more closely at their training and competitions, and to work on issues like fear of failure. They understand that writing can affect an athlete's physical and emotional well-being by reducing stress and anxiety, increasing self-awareness, sharpening mental skills, and strengthening coping abilities. Writing also complements other psychological techniques like meditation and visualization.

Throughout the *Soccer Team Notebook*, your athletes (and you, if you choose to write) will analyze, process, and reflect on practices, games, and life on and off of the pitch. There are countless ways to use the sections of this notebook. Here's one example:

After watching a match, have your players complete a Game Analysis II. At the next practice, ask players to divide up into small groups and discuss their analyses for a few minutes. Then, bring the small groups together for a full team discussion of each group's observations. The same activity can be done with other sections of the book. Small and large group discussions give most players an opportunity to talk, share ideas, and learn.

If you collect notebooks to review during the season, you may want to jot notes to your players in "Coach's Comments" at the back of the book. But, that's totally up to you. We do know that you'll learn more about your players—and your team—by reading the notebooks at some point during the season.

There are many ways to learn as an athlete; writing is one of them. "We write not to say what we know," said Pulitzer Prize winner Donald Murray, "but to learn, to discover, to know." This is to say that writing is a powerful way to learn, and that's why scientists, historians, and athletes keep notebooks, logs, and journals.

Finally, we suggest that you read *Writing on the Bus: Using Athletic Team Notebooks and Journals to Advance Learning and Performance in Sports* (2012). This book offers practical examples for using team notebooks and presents the theories that support the use of writing as way to learn in athletics.

We also invite you to check out our resource website at WritingAthletes.com. Very best wishes to you and your team.

Richard Kent   Amy Edwards
Orono, Maine   *Spokane, Washington*

Preseason Thoughts

"We are what we repeatedly do. Excellence, therefore, is not an act, but a habit."

—Aristotle

Preseason Thoughts

What were your strengths last season as a soccer player?

- defending- helping as a defensive
  midfielder
- winning balls out of the air
  using all surfaces

Last season, in what areas did your playing skills need to improve?

- supporting teammates when
  off the ball (showing)
- scoring off of free kicks
  outside the box
- getting more involved in the attack

In the offseason, what did you do to improve as a soccer player?

- extra training
- work on free kicks outside the box
- endurance/ running

Write about and describe your most satisfying performance last season during a match or a training session. What contributed to this performance?

- Game vs Desert Vista
  - win over one of the top teams in
    the state of a higher division
  - worked together and proved we
    have what it takes to win a
    state championships

Write about and describe your most disappointing performance from last season. What contributed to this performance?

- Presidents cup semi-final vs Premier
  - lost to a team we beat earlier in the season
  - My right knee was in pain because of my knee tracking thing

What are your Personal Athletic Goals for this season? A personal goal is not "I'm going to score 7 goals this season." A personal goal is a specific performance objective you plan to accomplish. Perhaps you plan to improve your juggling, free kicks for accuracy, or penalty kicks. Your entry might look like this one:

Personal Athletic Goals	What will you do to reach your Personal Athletic Goals?	Who might help you reach these goals?
–Increase my personal best at juggling on all surfaces.	–I have juggled at home for 10 minutes a day. I'm increasing to 15 minutes a day plus 30 minutes on one weekend day.	–My little brother Bailey will juggle with me and that makes it fun.

Personal Athletic Goals	What will you do to reach your Personal Athletic Goals?	Who might help you reach these goals?
1. Increase my free kick avg to 90%.	1. Stay after practice to work on it/on off days	1. My dad can help me get more reps by fetching balls
2. attack more/ take on players, 1v1s	2. Do it more often, take a risk sometimes	2. My team-mates, by being defenders
3. Become good captain material talk!	3. talk to my teammates, read	3. Myself, get out of my comfort zone

12

Last year our team strengths included the following:

- individual skill
- getting down the field

Last year our team needed to work more in the following areas:

- working toghether
- consistency

Write about and describe the most satisfying team performance last season during a match or a training session. What contributed to this performance?

Game vs Desert Vista
see page 11

Write about and describe the most disappointing team performance from last season. What contributed to this performance?

- League Game vs Blackhawks
  - everyone was arguing with the refs and opponents
  - teammates were fighting with each other on the field

What do you believe this year's team strengths will be?

- the ability to win games
- building from the back
- keeping possession

In what areas will this year's team need to improve?

- Finishing opportunities when we create them
- trust/team unity

Final thoughts on the upcoming season:

I'm very excited

Notes

Midseason Thoughts

"To watch people push themselves further than they think they can, it's a beautiful thing. It's really human."

—Abby Wambach

Midseason Thoughts

What are your strengths so far this season as a soccer player?

In what areas do you need to improve?

What's your most significant accomplishment so far this season?

Write about your best personal performance so far this season. What contributed to your success?

Write about your worst performance so far this season. What contributed to your poor play? How did you rebound from that performance?

So far this season our team strengths include...

Our team needs to improve in the following areas...

Personal Athletic Goals

Go back to the three Personal Athletic Goals that you established at the beginning of this workbook. List them below. Rank your effectiveness in each on the numeric chart.

Goal 1: _____

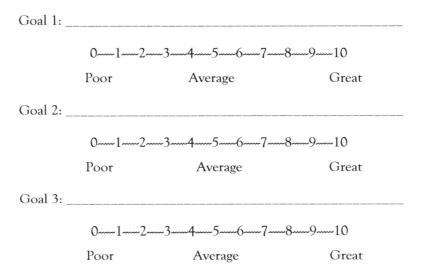

0——1——2——3——4——5——6——7——8——9——10

Poor   Average   Great

Goal 2: _____

0——1——2——3——4——5——6——7——8——9——10

Poor   Average   Great

Goal 3: _____

0——1——2——3——4——5——6——7——8——9——10

Poor   Average   Great

What specific work or activities are you doing to pursue these goals?

If you believe you are being successful in pursuing these goals, how do you know this? What evidence is there?

Midseason Letter

Write a letter about your performance thus far to your coach, a teammate... or to *yourself*.

Postseason Thoughts

"In the end, it's extra effort that separates a winner from second place. But winning takes a lot more than that, too. It starts with complete command of the fundamentals. Then it takes desire, determination, discipline, and self-sacrifice. And, finally, it takes a great deal of love, fairness and respect for your fellow man. Put all these together, and even if you don't win, how can you lose?"

–Jesse Owens

Postseason Thoughts

What have been your strengths this season as a soccer player?

What areas still need improvement?

What has been your most significant accomplishment this season?

Write about your best personal performance this season in a match or training session. What contributed to your success?

Write about your worst performance this season in a match or training session. What contributed to this performance? How did you rebound from that performance?

This season our team strengths included...

Our team still needed to work on the following areas...

What are your plans in the offseason for training?

Personal Athletic Goals

Go back to the three Personal Athletic Goals that you established at the beginning of this workbook. List and rank your effectiveness below.

Goal 1: _____

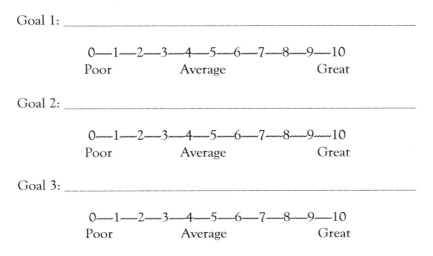

0~~1~~2~~3~~4~~5~~6~~7~~8~~9~~10
Poor   Average   Great

Goal 2: _____

0~~1~~2~~3~~4~~5~~6~~7~~8~~9~~10
Poor   Average   Great

Goal 3: _____

0~~1~~2~~3~~4~~5~~6~~7~~8~~9~~10
Poor   Average   Great

What did you do to be successful in pursuing these goals?

If you were successful, how do you know this? What evidence is there?

In what areas do you need to improve to achieve any of these goals in the future?

Match Analysis I

Instructions for *Match Analysis I*

The prompts on these pages provide you with an opportunity to analyze your match. Unpacking a soccer game in this fashion, whether you were a reserve or played every minute, helps you think more objectively while seeing the larger picture of a game. This thinking will help you improve your understanding of soccer. The *MAI* may be used for scrimmages, *friendlies*, and intrasquad contests as well as your league or conference matches.

When you fill out an *MAI*, don't be overly concerned about the conventions of writing. In other words, don't worry about spelling, grammar, and paragraphing... *just write*.

Checkout the model *MAI* on the next page and look closely at the way the player addressed certain prompts. But remember, these are just models—you'll have your own way of telling the story of a match.

In the final section of the *MAI*, you'll see a Player Check-in. This section can usually be accomplished quickly. Don't sit around and ponder life. Give a general response that reflects your immediate thought. Rate each topic in the Player Check-in using the following scale:

Above Average (+)   Average (O)   Below Average (−)

As you go through these topics, focus on the following:

Health: How's my over all health?

Sleep: Am I getting enough sleep each night?

Hydration: Do I take in enough water throughout the day as well as before, during, and after a match?

Fitness: How's my overall fitness level?

Nutrition: The USDA has a basic informational Website that offers nutritional guidance about the consumption of food (see ChooseMyPlate.Gov). For purposes of the Player Check-in, ask yourself whether you've eaten the suggested foods of a healthy diet (i.e., grains, proteins, veggies, fruit).

If you have further questions about the *MAI*, ask your coach. If you have questions, you can bet several of your teammates do, too.

-MODEL-

 ## Match Analysis I

Opponent: *Leavitt* (W 3 L 1 D 0) Date: *9/18* Result: *1-0 W* Pitch: *Home*
Record: Wins: 4 Losses: 0 Draws: 0   Minutes Played: 88 minutes

- My strengths as a player in today's match:

  Maintained defense's compactness. Right amount of talk–I didn't talk too much like at Lisbon. I had a <u>brilliant</u> run through the midfield into the attacking third... ☺

- My weaknesses as a player in today's match:

  I could have been more supportive of Jason. When I encourage him he plays better.

- Team strengths in today's match:

  We worked as a team–great support–positive comments... Good halftime adjustments.

- Team weaknesses in today's match:

  We could have been more inventive in attack during the 2ⁿᵈ half. We used Matt too much.

- Opponent's strengths:

  LHS never let down. #9 had warp-speed. His runs opened space and chances on goal.

- Opponent's weaknesses:

  Their midfielders and forwards did not mark us well in attack.

- What was the "difference" in today's match:

  Our midfielders' support of the forwards...and, did I mention, a brilliant run by the sweeper?

- What team adjustment would you suggest for the next match against this opponent?

  #9=FAST. Move Dusty? More variety in attack.

- Who was the Player of the Match and why?

  Ryan's save in the second half kept the match at 1-0. He came out bravely, as you would say, and took the ball off the offender's foot.

– Other comments (e.g., team strategy, attitude, preparation....)

We were prepared! The seniors had us ready to play.
Un-DE-feated!

Player Check-in

Above Average (+)   Average (O)   Below Average (–)

Health   +   *Nutrition:* Grains   O

Sleep   O   Protein   +

Hydration O   Veggies   –

Fitness   +   Fruit   O

Life Beyond Soccer O

Quotable Quote: *"The guy's not human!" by Dusty about #9 LHS*

 *Match Analysis I*

Opponent: _____(W ___ L ___ D___) *Date:* ____ Result:____ Pitch: ____

Record: Wins: ___ Losses: ___ Draws: ___   Minutes Played: ____

−   My strengths as a player in today's match:

−   My weaknesses as a player in today's match:

−   Team strengths in today's match:

−   Team weaknesses in today's match:

−   Opponent's strengths:

−   Opponent's weaknesses:

–   What was the "difference" in today's match:

–   What team adjustment would you suggest for the next match against this opponent?

–   Who was the Player of the Match and why?

–   Other comments (e.g., team strategy, attitude, preparation....)

Player Check-in
Above Average (+)   Average (O)   Below Average (–)

Health   _____   *Nutrition:* Grains _____

Sleep   _____   Protein _____

Hydration _____   Veggies _____

Fitness   _____   Fruit   _____

Life Beyond Soccer _____

Quotable Quote: _____

_____

Match Analysis I

Opponent: _____(W ___ L ___ D___) *Date:* ____ Result:____ Pitch: ____

Record: Wins: ___ Losses: ___ Draws: ___   Minutes Played: ____

- My strengths as a player in today's match:

- My weaknesses as a player in today's match:

- Team strengths in today's match:

- Team weaknesses in today's match:

- Opponent's strengths:

- Opponent's weaknesses:

- What was the "difference" in today's match:

- What team adjustment would you suggest for the next match against this opponent?

- Who was the Player of the Match and why?

- Other comments (e.g., team strategy, attitude, preparation....)

Player Check-in
Above Average (+)   Average (O)   Below Average (–)

Health   _____   *Nutrition:* Grains _____

Sleep   _____   Protein _____

Hydration _____   Veggies _____

Fitness   _____   Fruit   _____

Life Beyond Soccer _____

Quotable Quote: _____

_____

Match Analysis I

Opponent: _____(W ___ L ___ D___) *Date:* ____ Result:____ Pitch: ____

Record: Wins: ___ Losses: ___ Draws: ___   Minutes Played: ____

- My strengths as a player in today's match:

- My weaknesses as a player in today's match:

- Team strengths in today's match:

- Team weaknesses in today's match:

- Opponent's strengths:

- Opponent's weaknesses:

– What was the "difference" in today's match:

– What team adjustment would you suggest for the next match against this opponent?

– Who was the Player of the Match and why?

– Other comments (e.g., team strategy, attitude, preparation....)

Player Check-in
Above Average (+)   Average (O)   Below Average (–)

Health   ____   *Nutrition:* Grains ____

Sleep   ____   Protein ____

Hydration ____   Veggies ____

Fitness ____   Fruit ____

Life Beyond Soccer ____

Quotable Quote: _____

_____

 *Match Analysis I*

Opponent: _____(W ___ L ___ D___) *Date:* ____ Result:____ Pitch: ____

Record: Wins: ___ Losses: ___ Draws: ___   Minutes Played: ____

-   My strengths as a player in today's match:

-   My weaknesses as a player in today's match:

-   Team strengths in today's match:

-   Team weaknesses in today's match:

-   Opponent's strengths:

-   Opponent's weaknesses:

– What was the "difference" in today's match:

– What team adjustment would you suggest for the next match against this opponent?

– Who was the Player of the Match and why?

– Other comments (e.g., team strategy, attitude, preparation....)

Player Check-in
Above Average (+)   Average (O)   Below Average (−)

Health   ____   *Nutrition:* Grains ____

Sleep   ____   Protein ____

Hydration ____   Veggies ____

Fitness   ____   Fruit ____

Life Beyond Soccer ____

Quotable Quote: _____

_____

 *Match Analysis I*

Opponent: _____(W ___ L ___ D___) *Date:* ____ Result:____ Pitch: ____

Record: Wins: ___ Losses: ___ Draws: ___   Minutes Played: ____

–   My strengths as a player in today's match:

–   My weaknesses as a player in today's match:

–   Team strengths in today's match:

–   Team weaknesses in today's match:

–   Opponent's strengths:

–   Opponent's weaknesses:

–   What was the "difference" in today's match:

–   What team adjustment would you suggest for the next match against this
    opponent?

–   Who was the Player of the Match and why?

–   Other comments (e.g., team strategy, attitude, preparation....)

Player Check-in
Above Average (+)   Average (O)   Below Average (–)

Health _____

Sleep _____

Hydration _____

Fitness _____

Nutrition: Grains _____

Protein _____

Veggies _____

Fruit _____

Life Beyond Soccer _____

Quotable Quote: _____

_____

 *Match Analysis I*

Opponent: _____(W ___ L ___ D___) *Date:* ____ Result:____ Pitch: ____

Record: Wins: ___ Losses: ___ Draws: ___   Minutes Played: ____

- My strengths as a player in today's match:

- My weaknesses as a player in today's match:

- Team strengths in today's match:

- Team weaknesses in today's match:

- Opponent's strengths:

- Opponent's weaknesses:

–   What was the "difference" in today's match:

–   What team adjustment would you suggest for the next match against this opponent?

–   Who was the Player of the Match and why?

–   Other comments (e.g., team strategy, attitude, preparation....)

Player Check-in
Above Average (+)   Average (O)   Below Average (–)

Health   _____   *Nutrition:* Grains _____

Sleep   _____   Protein _____

Hydration _____   Veggies _____

Fitness   _____   Fruit   _____

Life Beyond Soccer _____

Quotable Quote: _____

_____

 *Match Analysis I*

Opponent: _____(W ___ L ___ D___) *Date:* ____ Result:____ Pitch: ____

Record: Wins: ___ Losses: ___ Draws: ___   Minutes Played: ____

- My strengths as a player in today's match:

- My weaknesses as a player in today's match:

- Team strengths in today's match:

- Team weaknesses in today's match:

- Opponent's strengths:

- Opponent's weaknesses:

- What was the "difference" in today's match:

- What team adjustment would you suggest for the next match against this opponent?

- Who was the Player of the Match and why?

- Other comments (e.g., team strategy, attitude, preparation....)

Player Check-in
Above Average (+)   Average (O)   Below Average (–)

Health _____   *Nutrition:* Grains _____

Sleep _____   Protein _____

Hydration _____   Veggies _____

Fitness _____   Fruit _____

Life Beyond Soccer _____

Quotable Quote: _____

_____

 *Match Analysis I*

Opponent: _____(W ___ L ___ D___) *Date:* ____ Result:____ Pitch: ____

Record: Wins: ___ Losses: ___ Draws: ___   Minutes Played: ____

- My strengths as a player in today's match:

- My weaknesses as a player in today's match:

- Team strengths in today's match:

- Team weaknesses in today's match:

- Opponent's strengths:

- Opponent's weaknesses:

- What was the "difference" in today's match:

- What team adjustment would you suggest for the next match against this opponent?

- Who was the Player of the Match and why?

- Other comments (e.g., team strategy, attitude, preparation....)

Player Check-in
Above Average (+)   Average (O)   Below Average (–)

Health _____		*Nutrition:* Grains _____
Sleep _____		Protein _____
Hydration _____		Veggies _____
Fitness _____		Fruit _____

Life Beyond Soccer _____

Quotable Quote: _____

_____

 *Match Analysis I*

Opponent: _____(W ___ L ___ D___) *Date:* ____ Result:____ Pitch: ____

Record: Wins: ___ Losses: ___ Draws: ___   Minutes Played: ____

- My strengths as a player in today's match:

- My weaknesses as a player in today's match:

- Team strengths in today's match:

- Team weaknesses in today's match:

- Opponent's strengths:

- Opponent's weaknesses:

– What was the "difference" in today's match:

– What team adjustment would you suggest for the next match against this opponent?

– Who was the Player of the Match and why?

– Other comments (e.g., team strategy, attitude, preparation....)

Player Check-in
Above Average (+)   Average (O)   Below Average (–)

Health   _____   *Nutrition:* Grains _____

Sleep   _____   Protein _____

Hydration _____   Veggies _____

Fitness   _____   Fruit   _____

Life Beyond Soccer _____

Quotable Quote: _____

_____

 *Match Analysis I*

Opponent: _____(W ___ L ___ D___) *Date:* ____ Result:____ Pitch: ____

Record: Wins: ___ Losses: ___ Draws: ___   Minutes Played: ____

- My strengths as a player in today's match:

- My weaknesses as a player in today's match:

- Team strengths in today's match:

- Team weaknesses in today's match:

- Opponent's strengths:

- Opponent's weaknesses:

- What was the "difference" in today's match:

- What team adjustment would you suggest for the next match against this opponent?

- Who was the Player of the Match and why?

- Other comments (e.g., team strategy, attitude, preparation....)

Player Check-in

Above Average (+)   Average (O)   Below Average (–)

Health   _____   *Nutrition:* Grains _____

Sleep   _____   Protein _____

Hydration _____   Veggies _____

Fitness   _____   Fruit   _____

Life Beyond Soccer _____

Quotable Quote: _____

_____

 *Match Analysis I*

Opponent: _____(W ___ L ___ D___) *Date:* ____ Result:____ Pitch: ____

Record: Wins: ___ Losses: ___ Draws: ___   Minutes Played: ____

– My strengths as a player in today's match:

– My weaknesses as a player in today's match:

– Team strengths in today's match:

– Team weaknesses in today's match:

– Opponent's strengths:

– Opponent's weaknesses:

– What was the "difference" in today's match:

– What team adjustment would you suggest for the next match against this opponent?

– Who was the Player of the Match and why?

– Other comments (e.g., team strategy, attitude, preparation....)

Player Check-in
Above Average (+)   Average (O)   Below Average (–)

Health _____   *Nutrition:* Grains _____

Sleep _____   Protein _____

Hydration _____   Veggies _____

Fitness _____   Fruit _____

Life Beyond Soccer _____

Quotable Quote: _____

_____

Match Analysis I

Opponent: _____(W ___ L ___ D___) *Date:* ____ Result:____ Pitch: ____

Record: Wins: ___ Losses: ___ Draws: ___   Minutes Played: ____

- My strengths as a player in today's match:

- My weaknesses as a player in today's match:

- Team strengths in today's match:

- Team weaknesses in today's match:

- Opponent's strengths:

- Opponent's weaknesses:

– What was the "difference" in today's match:

– What team adjustment would you suggest for the next match against this opponent?

– Who was the Player of the Match and why?

– Other comments (e.g., team strategy, attitude, preparation....)

Player Check-in
Above Average (+)   Average (O)   Below Average (–)

Health   _____

Nutrition: Grains _____

Sleep   _____

Protein _____

Hydration _____

Veggies _____

Fitness   _____

Fruit   _____

Life Beyond Soccer _____

Quotable Quote: _____

_____

 *Match Analysis I*

Opponent: _____(W ___ L ___ D___) *Date:* ____ Result:____ Pitch: ____

Record: Wins: ___ Losses: ___ Draws: ___   Minutes Played: ____

- My strengths as a player in today's match:

- My weaknesses as a player in today's match:

- Team strengths in today's match:

- Team weaknesses in today's match:

- Opponent's strengths:

- Opponent's weaknesses:

- What was the "difference" in today's match:

- What team adjustment would you suggest for the next match against this opponent?

- Who was the Player of the Match and why?

- Other comments (e.g., team strategy, attitude, preparation....)

Player Check-in
Above Average (+)   Average (O)   Below Average (–)

Health _____   *Nutrition:* Grains _____

Sleep _____   Protein _____

Hydration _____   Veggies _____

Fitness _____   Fruit _____

Life Beyond Soccer _____

Quotable Quote: _____

_____

 *Match Analysis I*

Opponent: _____(W ___ L ___ D___) *Date:* ____ Result:____ Pitch: ____

Record: Wins: ___ Losses: ___ Draws: ___   Minutes Played: ____

– My strengths as a player in today's match:

– My weaknesses as a player in today's match:

– Team strengths in today's match:

– Team weaknesses in today's match:

– Opponent's strengths:

– Opponent's weaknesses:

– What was the "difference" in today's match:

– What team adjustment would you suggest for the next match against this opponent?

– Who was the Player of the Match and why?

– Other comments (e.g., team strategy, attitude, preparation....)

Player Check-in
Above Average (+)   Average (O)   Below Average (–)

Health   _____   *Nutrition:* Grains _____

Sleep   _____   Protein _____

Hydration _____   Veggies _____

Fitness   _____   Fruit   _____

Life Beyond Soccer _____

Quotable Quote: _____

_____

 *Match Analysis I*

Opponent: _____ (W ___ L ___ D ___) *Date:* ____ Result: ____ Pitch: ____

Record: Wins: ___ Losses: ___ Draws: ___   Minutes Played: ____

- My strengths as a player in today's match:

- My weaknesses as a player in today's match:

- Team strengths in today's match:

- Team weaknesses in today's match:

- Opponent's strengths:

- Opponent's weaknesses:

- What was the "difference" in today's match:

- What team adjustment would you suggest for the next match against this opponent?

- Who was the Player of the Match and why?

- Other comments (e.g., team strategy, attitude, preparation....)

Player Check-in

Above Average (+)   Average (O)   Below Average (–)

Health   _____   *Nutrition:* Grains _____

Sleep   _____   Protein _____

Hydration _____   Veggies _____

Fitness   _____   Fruit   _____

Life Beyond Soccer _____

Quotable Quote: _____

_____

Match Analysis I

Opponent: _____(W ___ L ___ D___) *Date:* ____ Result:____ Pitch: ____

Record: Wins: ___ Losses: ___ Draws: ___   Minutes Played: ____

- My strengths as a player in today's match:

- My weaknesses as a player in today's match:

- Team strengths in today's match:

- Team weaknesses in today's match:

- Opponent's strengths:

- Opponent's weaknesses:

– What was the "difference" in today's match:

– What team adjustment would you suggest for the next match against this opponent?

– Who was the Player of the Match and why?

– Other comments (e.g., team strategy, attitude, preparation....)

Player Check-in
Above Average (+)   Average (O)   Below Average (–)

Health   _____   *Nutrition:* Grains _____

Sleep   _____   Protein _____

Hydration _____   Veggies _____

Fitness   _____   Fruit _____

Life Beyond Soccer _____

Quotable Quote: _____

_____

 *Match Analysis I*

Opponent: _____(W ___ L ___ D___) *Date:* ____ Result:____ Pitch: ____

Record: Wins: ___ Losses: ___ Draws: ___   Minutes Played: ____

- My strengths as a player in today's match:

- My weaknesses as a player in today's match:

- Team strengths in today's match:

- Team weaknesses in today's match:

- Opponent's strengths:

- Opponent's weaknesses:

- What was the "difference" in today's match:

- What team adjustment would you suggest for the next match against this opponent?

- Who was the Player of the Match and why?

- Other comments (e.g., team strategy, attitude, preparation....)

Player Check-in

Above Average (+)   Average (O)   Below Average (–)

Health _____   *Nutrition:* Grains _____

Sleep _____   Protein _____

Hydration _____   Veggies _____

Fitness _____   Fruit _____

Life Beyond Soccer _____

Quotable Quote: _____

_____

 *Match Analysis I*

Opponent: _____(W ___ L ___ D___) *Date:* ____ Result:____ Pitch: ____

Record: Wins: ___ Losses: ___ Draws: ___   Minutes Played: ____

- My strengths as a player in today's match:

- My weaknesses as a player in today's match:

- Team strengths in today's match:

- Team weaknesses in today's match:

- Opponent's strengths:

- Opponent's weaknesses:

–   What was the "difference" in today's match:

–   What team adjustment would you suggest for the next match against this
    opponent?

–   Who was the Player of the Match and why?

–   Other comments (e.g., team strategy, attitude, preparation....)

Player Check-in
Above Average (+)   Average (O)   Below Average (–)

Health   ____   *Nutrition:* Grains ____

Sleep   ____   Protein ____

Hydration ____   Veggies ____

Fitness   ____   Fruit   ____

Life Beyond Soccer ____

Quotable Quote: _____

_____

 *Match Analysis I*

Opponent: _____(W ___ L ___ D___) *Date:* ____ Result:____ Pitch: ____

Record: Wins: ___ Losses: ___ Draws: ___   Minutes Played: ____

- My strengths as a player in today's match:

- My weaknesses as a player in today's match:

- Team strengths in today's match:

- Team weaknesses in today's match:

- Opponent's strengths:

- Opponent's weaknesses:

- What was the "difference" in today's match:

- What team adjustment would you suggest for the next match against this opponent?

- Who was the Player of the Match and why?

- Other comments (e.g., team strategy, attitude, preparation....)

Player Check-in
Above Average (+)   Average (O)   Below Average (–)

Health   ____   *Nutrition:* Grains ____

Sleep   ____   Protein ____

Hydration ____   Veggies ____

Fitness   ____   Fruit   ____

Life Beyond Soccer ____

Quotable Quote: _____

_____

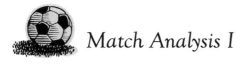

Match Analysis I

Opponent: _____(W ___ L ___ D___) *Date:* ____ Result:____ Pitch: ____

Record: Wins: ___ Losses: ___ Draws: ___   Minutes Played: ____

–   My strengths as a player in today's match:

–   My weaknesses as a player in today's match:

–   Team strengths in today's match:

–   Team weaknesses in today's match:

–   Opponent's strengths:

–   Opponent's weaknesses:

- What was the "difference" in today's match:

- What team adjustment would you suggest for the next match against this opponent?

- Who was the Player of the Match and why?

- Other comments (e.g., team strategy, attitude, preparation....)

Player Check-in
Above Average (+)   Average (O)   Below Average (–)

Health ____   *Nutrition:* Grains ____

Sleep ____   Protein ____

Hydration ____   Veggies ____

Fitness ____   Fruit ____

Life Beyond Soccer ____

Quotable Quote: _____

_____

 *Match Analysis I*

Opponent: _____(W ___ L ___ D___)   *Date:* ____   Result:____   Pitch: ____

Record: Wins: ___ Losses: ___ Draws: ___   Minutes Played: ____

- My strengths as a player in today's match:

- My weaknesses as a player in today's match:

- Team strengths in today's match:

- Team weaknesses in today's match:

- Opponent's strengths:

- Opponent's weaknesses:

- What was the "difference" in today's match:

- What team adjustment would you suggest for the next match against this opponent?

- Who was the Player of the Match and why?

- Other comments (e.g., team strategy, attitude, preparation....)

Player Check-in
Above Average (+)   Average (O)   Below Average (−)

Health ____   *Nutrition:* Grains ____

Sleep ____   Protein ____

Hydration ____   Veggies ____

Fitness ____   Fruit ____

Life Beyond Soccer ____

Quotable Quote: _____

_____

 *Match Analysis I*

Opponent: _____(W ___ L ___ D___) *Date:* ____ Result:____ Pitch: ____

Record: Wins: ___ Losses: ___ Draws: ___   Minutes Played: ____

- My strengths as a player in today's match:

- My weaknesses as a player in today's match:

- Team strengths in today's match:

- Team weaknesses in today's match:

- Opponent's strengths:

- Opponent's weaknesses:

- What was the "difference" in today's match:

- What team adjustment would you suggest for the next match against this opponent?

- Who was the Player of the Match and why?

- Other comments (e.g., team strategy, attitude, preparation....)

Player Check-in
Above Average (+)   Average (O)   Below Average (–)

Health   _____   *Nutrition:* Grains _____

Sleep   _____   Protein _____

Hydration _____   Veggies _____

Fitness   _____   Fruit   _____

Life Beyond Soccer _____

Quotable Quote: _____

_____

Match Analysis I

Opponent: _____(W ___ L ___ D___) *Date:* ____ Result:____ Pitch: ____

Record: Wins: ___ Losses: ___ Draws: ___   Minutes Played: ____

- My strengths as a player in today's match:

- My weaknesses as a player in today's match:

- Team strengths in today's match:

- Team weaknesses in today's match:

- Opponent's strengths:

- Opponent's weaknesses:

- What was the "difference" in today's match:

- What team adjustment would you suggest for the next match against this opponent?

- Who was the Player of the Match and why?

- Other comments (e.g., team strategy, attitude, preparation....)

Player Check-in
Above Average (+)   Average (O)   Below Average (–)

Health   _____   *Nutrition:* Grains _____

Sleep   _____   Protein _____

Hydration _____   Veggies _____

Fitness   _____   Fruit   _____

Life Beyond Soccer _____

Quotable Quote: _____

_____

 *Match Analysis I*

Opponent: _____(W ___ L ___ D___)   *Date:* ____   Result:____   Pitch: ____

Record: Wins: ___ Losses: ___ Draws: ___   Minutes Played: ____

- My strengths as a player in today's match:

- My weaknesses as a player in today's match:

- Team strengths in today's match:

- Team weaknesses in today's match:

- Opponent's strengths:

- Opponent's weaknesses:

- What was the "difference" in today's match:

- What team adjustment would you suggest for the next match against this opponent?

- Who was the Player of the Match and why?

- Other comments (e.g., team strategy, attitude, preparation....)

Player Check-in
Above Average (+)   Average (O)   Below Average (–)

Health   ____   *Nutrition:* Grains ____

Sleep   ____   Protein ____

Hydration ____   Veggies ____

Fitness   ____   Fruit   ____

Life Beyond Soccer ____

Quotable Quote: _____

_____

 *Match Analysis I*

Opponent: _____(W ___ L ___ D___) *Date:* ____ Result:____ Pitch: ____

Record: Wins: ___ Losses: ___ Draws: ___   Minutes Played: ____

- My strengths as a player in today's match:

- My weaknesses as a player in today's match:

- Team strengths in today's match:

- Team weaknesses in today's match:

- Opponent's strengths:

- Opponent's weaknesses:

- What was the "difference" in today's match:

- What team adjustment would you suggest for the next match against this opponent?

- Who was the Player of the Match and why?

- Other comments (e.g., team strategy, attitude, preparation....)

Player Check-in
Above Average (+)   Average (O)   Below Average (–)

Health   _____   *Nutrition:* Grains _____

Sleep   _____   Protein _____

Hydration _____   Veggies _____

Fitness   _____   Fruit   _____

Life Beyond Soccer _____

Quotable Quote: _____

_____

Match Analysis II

Instructions for *Match Analyses II*

Throughout the soccer season, you'll have opportunities to analyze matches that you've watched in person, on TV, or online. Filling out the *Match Analysis II* can help you look more objectively at those games. The *MAII* is a learning activity that will challenge you to watch a match more critically, more fully, and more like a coach than an athlete. Unpacking a soccer match with the *Match Analysis II* will guide you to becoming a more thoughtful student of the game.

-MODEL-

 Match Analysis II

Team #1 Torrence HS

Wins: 6 Losses: 4 Draws: 2

Date: *September 29*

Alignment of Players:
4-4-2

Strengths:
*Outside midfielders
made great runs.*

Weaknesses:
*They seemed to relax
when they were up 2-0.
Young.*

Half-time adjustments & effects:
*None. They came
out flat. Over confident.*

Team #2 Freedom HS

Wins: 7 Losses: 3 Draws: 1

Pitch: *Freedom*

Alignment of Players:
1ˢᵗ half   4-4-2   2ⁿᵈ: 4-3-3

Strengths:
*Sweeper
Center Mid*

Weaknesses:
*Didn't use space well.
Their coach: a screamer.*

Half-time adjustments & effects:
*Went to a 4-3-3 for more
targets up front. Created
more opportunities.*

General Comments:

Forwards
Fast

Midfielders
Athletic

Defenders
Moved well together.

Keeper
*Confident—great technique—
team leader.*

Forwards
Lacked movement

Midfielders
*Lost composure—their talk was
not constructive.*

Defenders
Seemed spacey. Lost track of play.

Keeper
*Poor positioning.
No Talk. Lost it after 2ⁿᵈ goal.*

Player of the Match:

#6—left mid. His runs through the D opened up huge space. He always encouraged his mates. He's the kind of player I'd like to be. Great goal.

Sweeper—he kept his cool. It's not easy managing younger players.

Moment of the Match:

#6's run through the D and his one-touch to the near post. Sweet String Music! Magic!

Final Analysis:

THS needed to work on the simple things: move to space and play the way you face. They were a lot younger than FHS and just needed to try to play within themselves. It's like you told us over the last two years. Play the fundamentals—it's a simple game so keep it that way. As for FHS, they didn't stay focused for the whole match. Their coach needed to teach not yell—the guy embarrassed himself.

Match Analysis II

Team #1_____ v. Team #2_____

Wins: _____ Losses: _____ Draws: _____   Wins: _____ Losses: _____ Draws: _____

Date: _____   Pitch: _____

Alignment of Players: Alignment of Players:

Strengths: Strengths:

Weaknesses: Weaknesses:

Half-time adjustments & effects: Half-time adjustments & effects:

General Comments:

Forwards   Forwards

Midfielders   Midfielders

Defenders   Defenders

Keeper   Keeper

Players of the Match:

Moment of the Match:

Final Analysis:

Match Analysis II

Team #1_____ v. Team #2_____

Wins: _____ Losses: _____ Draws: _____   Wins: _____ Losses: _____ Draws: _____

Date: _____   Pitch: _____

Alignment of Players: Alignment of Players:

Strengths: Strengths:

Weaknesses: Weaknesses:

Half-time adjustments & effects: Half-time adjustments & effects:

General Comments:

Forwards   Forwards

Midfielders   Midfielders

Defenders   Defenders

Keeper   Keeper

Players of the Match:

Moment of the Match:

Final Analysis:

Match Analysis II

Team #1_____ v. Team #2_____

Wins: _____ Losses: _____ Draws: _____   Wins: _____ Losses: _____ Draws: _____

Date: _____   Pitch: _____

Alignment of Players: Alignment of Players:

Strengths: Strengths:

Weaknesses: Weaknesses:

Half-time adjustments & effects: Half-time adjustments & effects:

General Comments:

Forwards   Forwards

Midfielders   Midfielders

Defenders   Defenders

Keeper   Keeper

Players of the Match:

Moment of the Match:

Final Analysis:

Match Analysis II

Team #1_____ v. Team #2_____

Wins: _____ Losses: _____ Draws: _____   Wins: _____ Losses: _____ Draws: _____

Date: _____   Pitch: _____

Alignment of Players: Alignment of Players:

Strengths: Strengths:

Weaknesses: Weaknesses:

Half-time adjustments & effects: Half-time adjustments & effects:

General Comments:

Forwards   Forwards

Midfielders   Midfielders

Defenders   Defenders

Keeper   Keeper

Players of the Match:

Moment of the Match:

Final Analysis:

Match Analysis II

Team #1_____ v. Team #2_____

Wins: ____ Losses: ____ Draws: ____   Wins: ____ Losses: ____ Draws: ____

Date: _____   Pitch: _____

Alignment of Players: Alignment of Players:

Strengths: Strengths:

Weaknesses: Weaknesses:

Half-time adjustments & effects: Half-time adjustments & effects:

General Comments:

Forwards   Forwards

Midfielders   Midfielders

Defenders   Defenders

Keeper   Keeper

Players of the Match:

Moment of the Match:

Final Analysis:

Performance Feedback

Instructions for *Performance Feedback*

At different times throughout the soccer season, your coach will ask you to fill out one of the following Performance Feedback forms immediately after a match. This form helps you look closely at the stress you experience before and during a game. As an athlete, writing about stressors can help you manage those feelings in the future.

You'll be asked to discuss your "self-talk." As you might guess, self-talk is the talking you do in your own head about yourself or during a training session or match. Often, self-talk happens without us even noticing. However, what you say to yourself before or during a match can impact the way that you feel and perform. Sports psychologists recognize the importance of positive self-talk in helping athletes achieve their potential.

-MODEL-

Performance Feedback*

Opponent: *UNB*   Date: *September 18*

What stressors did you experience before, during, and after this match?

Before the match I was concerned about the weather.

How did you experience this stress? Did it manifest in your thoughts, in the way you felt, or in the way you acted?

I worried that the weather would equalize play. We were definitely the better team and these thoughts made me—not nervous really, but a bit jittery.

Mark on this scale your level of excitement and motivation for the match.

```
0------------------------5-/------------------------10
   Too Low            Perfect            Too High
```

In a few words, describe your feelings at the various times in the day?

   Travel to match: *Excited*

   Warm up: *Pumped up*

   Just before the match: *Calm & focused*

   During the match: *It took me about 15 minutes to settle in.*

   After the match: *I felt like we earned the win.*

What techniques did you use to manage any stress you experienced? How effective were you in controlling this stress?

I talked to some of my teammates about the weather, not taking this team lightly, and how we needed to stay in control. I felt confident in my play and the team's once we kicked off. Talking to others helped me focus.

Describe how your stressors, excitement/motivation, and self-talk impacted your performance.

I think I was uneasy on the pitch for the first 15 minutes. Even before that, I wonder whether the way I talked to my teammates before the match may have made some of them nervous. I wanted to make them aware of the weather's influence... but maybe I just sounded nervous? Not sure. Otherwise, I felt ready for this match and settled in.

After unpacking your game-day mental state, what would you do differently to improve for the next match?

Maybe I sounded a bit hyper about the weather to my teammates. Again, not sure. I would think through my comments about the weather.

Additional Thoughts:

We won!

*Adapted from a design by Sheila Stawinski of the University of Vermont.

Performance Feedback*

Opponent: _____   Date: _____

What stressors did you experience before, during and after this match?

How did you experience this stress? Did it manifest in your thoughts, in the way you felt, or in the way you acted?

Mark on this scale your level of excitement and motivation for the match.

0—————————————5—————————————10
Too Low   Perfect   Too High

In a few words, describe your feelings at the various times in the day?

　　Travel to match:

　　Warm up:

　　Just before the match:

　　During the match:

　　After the match:

What techniques did you use to manage any stress you experienced? How effective were you in controlling this stress?

How was your self-talk? Positive, negative, thoughtful?

Describe how your stressors, excitement/motivation, and self-talk impacted your performance.

After unpacking your game-day mental state, what would you do differently to improve for the next match?

Additional Thoughts:

*Adapted from a design by Sheila Stawinski of the University of Vermont.

Performance Feedback*

Opponent: _____   Date: _____

What stressors did you experience before, during and after this match?

How did you experience this stress? Did it manifest in your thoughts, in the way you felt, or in the way you acted?

Mark on this scale your level of excitement and motivation for the match.

0~~~~~~~~~~~~~~~~~~~~~~~~~~~~~5~~~~~~~~~~~~~~~~~~~~~~~~~~10
Too Low   Perfect   Too High

In a few words, describe your feelings at the various times in the day?

Travel to match:

Warm up:

Just before the match:

During the match:

After the match:

What techniques did you use to manage any stress you experienced? How effective were you in controlling this stress?

How was your self-talk? Positive, negative, thoughtful?

Describe how your stressors, excitement/motivation, and self-talk impacted your performance.

After unpacking your game-day mental state, what would you do differently to improve for the next match?

Additional Thoughts:

*Adapted from a design by Sheila Stawinski of the University of Vermont.

Performance Feedback*

Opponent: _____   Date: _____

What stressors did you experience before, during and after this match?

How did you experience this stress? Did it manifest in your thoughts, in the way you felt, or in the way you acted?

Mark on this scale your level of excitement and motivation for the match.

$$0 \text{~~~~~~~~~~~~~~~~~~~~~~~~~} 5 \text{~~~~~~~~~~~~~~~~~~~~~~~} 10$$
Too Low   Perfect   Too High

In a few words, describe your feelings at the various times in the day?

Travel to match:

Warm up:

Just before the match:

During the match:

After the match:

What techniques did you use to manage any stress you experienced? How effective were you in controlling this stress?

How was your self-talk? Positive, negative, thoughtful?

Describe how your stressors, excitement/motivation, and self-talk impacted your performance.

After unpacking your game-day mental state, what would you do differently to improve for the next match?

Additional Thoughts:

*Adapted from a design by Sheila Stawinski of the University of Vermont.

Performance Feedback*

Opponent: _____   Date: _____

What stressors did you experience before, during and after this match?

How did you experience this stress? Did it manifest in your thoughts, in the way you felt, or in the way you acted?

Mark on this scale your level of excitement and motivation for the match.

```
0~~~~~~~~~~~~~~~~~~~~~~~~~~~5~~~~~~~~~~~~~~~~~~~~~~~~~10
  Too Low              Perfect              Too High
```

In a few words, describe your feelings at the various times in the day?

Travel to match:

Warm up:

Just before the match:

During the match:

After the match:

What techniques did you use to manage any stress you experienced? How effective were you in controlling this stress?

How was your self-talk? Positive, negative, thoughtful?

Describe how your stressors, excitement/motivation, and self-talk impacted your performance.

After unpacking your game-day mental state, what would you do differently to improve for the next match?

Additional Thoughts:

*Adapted from a design by Sheila Stawinski of the University of Vermont.

Performance Feedback*

Opponent: _____   Date: _____

What stressors did you experience before, during and after this match?

How did you experience this stress? Did it manifest in your thoughts, in the way you felt, or in the way you acted?

Mark on this scale your level of excitement and motivation for the match.

```
      0~~~~~~~~~~~~~~~~~~~~~~~~5~~~~~~~~~~~~~~~~~~~~10
      Too Low              Perfect              Too High
```

In a few words, describe your feelings at the various times in the day?

   Travel to match:

   Warm up:

   Just before the match:

   During the match:

   After the match:

What techniques did you use to manage any stress you experienced? How effective were you in controlling this stress?

How was your self-talk? Positive, negative, thoughtful?

Describe how your stressors, excitement/motivation, and self-talk impacted your performance.

After unpacking your game-day mental state, what would you do differently to improve for the next match?

Additional Thoughts:

*Adapted from a design by Sheila Stawinski of the University of Vermont.

Performance Feedback*

Opponent: _____   Date: _____

What stressors did you experience before, during and after this match?

How did you experience this stress? Did it manifest in your thoughts, in the way you felt, or in the way you acted?

Mark on this scale your level of excitement and motivation for the match.

$$0\text{~~~~~~~~~~~~~~~~~~~~~~~~~~}5\text{~~~~~~~~~~~~~~~~~~~~~~~~~}10$$
Too Low   Perfect   Too High

In a few words, describe your feelings at the various times in the day?

    Travel to match:

    Warm up:

    Just before the match:

    During the match:

    After the match:

What techniques did you use to manage any stress you experienced? How effective were you in controlling this stress?

How was your self-talk? Positive, negative, thoughtful?

Describe how your stressors, excitement/motivation, and self-talk impacted your performance.

After unpacking your game-day mental state, what would you do differently to improve for the next match?

Additional Thoughts:

*Adapted from a design by Sheila Stawinski of the University of Vermont.

110

Performance Feedback*

Opponent: _____   Date: _____

What stressors did you experience before, during and after this match?

How did you experience this stress? Did it manifest in your thoughts, in the way you felt, or in the way you acted?

Mark on this scale your level of excitement and motivation for the match.

```
0~~~~~~~~~~~~~~~~~~~~~~~~~~5~~~~~~~~~~~~~~~~~~~~~~~~~~10
Too Low                 Perfect                Too High
```

In a few words, describe your feelings at the various times in the day?

   Travel to match:

   Warm up:

   Just before the match:

   During the match:

   After the match:

What techniques did you use to manage any stress you experienced? How effective were you in controlling this stress?

How was your self-talk? Positive, negative, thoughtful?

Describe how your stressors, excitement/motivation, and self-talk impacted your performance.

After unpacking your game-day mental state, what would you do differently to improve for the next match?

Additional Thoughts:

*Adapted from a design by Sheila Stawinski of the University of Vermont.

Athletic Journals

"Keeping a journal of what's going on in your life is a good way to help you distill what's important and what's not."

~Martina Navratilova

Writing an *Athletic Journal*

An Athlete's Journal provides you with a place to set goals, reflect, grapple with issues, keep track of training ideas, and record results as well as plan, scheme, ponder, rant, question, draw, and celebrate. In England, 16-year-old soccer players who become apprentices to professional teams are required to keep a journal about training sessions, games, diet.... The plain fact is that taking a few minutes to write amplifies your learning. These journal prompts will engage you and your teammates in different ways. And that difference is the beauty of such a learning activity. Writing has the potential to offer a powerful difference for your team.

Here are a few suggestions about writing responses to Athletic Journals.

- *Just Write It.* Don't be overly concerned with perfect writing. In other words, don't stop to check spelling, correct grammar, or create perfect paragraphs.

- *Quick Write:* When you're responding to the prompts in this section of your Team Notebook, try a Quick Write: write nonstop for 3 to 6 minutes. Do not take your pen or pencil off the paper. Just keep writing. If your mind goes blank, make a list of words related to the topic until you start writing sentences again. Here's an example of a Quick Write by a player whose team lost to a lesser team. Notice the list of words in the middle:

> I don't like losing to a team we should have beaten. Last time this happened I felt empty inside and kind of sick. I think about the times I messed up during the match. I think about... **poor passes, times I didn't talk, moments when I lost focus, my emotions, referee decisions, teammates' mistakes, anger...** I know my poor passes often happen because I'm not calm enough on the field. I've got to slow down my thinking. Same thing happens with my talk—I get too caught up in the moment of the game and forget to communicate to my teammates. It all comes down to my lack of focus when I let my emotions get the best of me. That's especially true when a referee makes a call I disagree with and I get angry and lose focus. I also get mad when a teammate messes up. I need to stay in the game—I need to slow things down in my mind.

- *Draw or sketch.* There are many ways to tell the story of your training and competing. Even if you can barely sketch stick figures, give drawing a try.

- *Word Web.* If you struggle to write one of the prompts in this workbook, try making a Word Web. Check out the example in Figure 1. Place the athletic writing prompt in the middle of the page and then list words that connect to the topic. Once you have 8-10 words, start writing about each word. You'll be surprised how your thoughts flow.

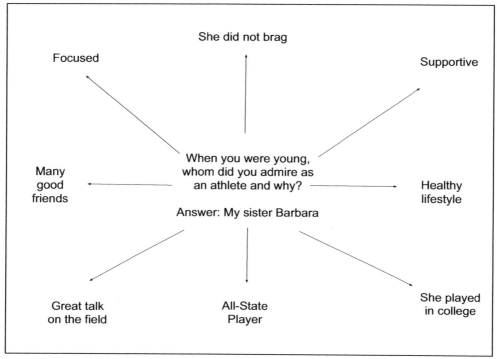

Figure 1 Word Web

Training

What makes training hard for you?

What makes training easy for you?

Your Timeline as a Soccer Player

Create a timeline of your soccer career. Include your athletic milestones, important coaches, and various teams. Write above and below the timeline.

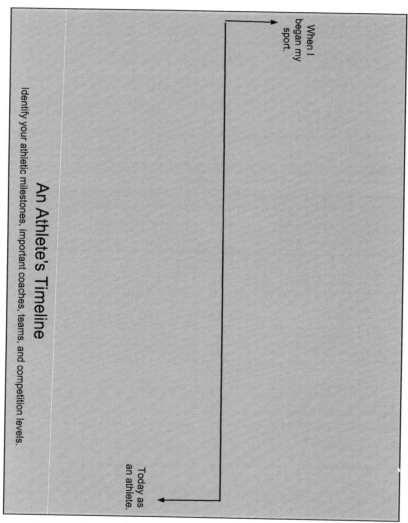

When I began my sport.

An Athlete's Timeline

Identify your athletic milestones, important coaches, teams, and competition levels.

Today as an athlete.

What's one thing you've noticed or thought about while filling out this timeline?

An Effective Coach

List up to five qualities of an effective coach:

1. _____

2. _____

3. _____

4. _____

5. _____

Tell the story of a good moment during a match or training session with one of your coaches:

The Perfect Warm-Up

Outline what you consider a perfect warm-up routine for a training session. Include the approximate amount of time spent on each activity, and the reason you have included this activity.

Warm-up activity	Time	Why this activity?

Write about a favorite teammate or training partner.

Teammate's/Training Partner's Name_____

Qualities as an athlete:

Qualities as a person:

Unique habits or quirks:

Best story about this teammate:

What have you learned from this athlete?

Who brings out your best and why?

Who brings out the best in you as an athlete and why? You might first think of a coach, manager, or trainer. But also think about family members, fans, teammates, or even an opponent.

Making Meaning Activity: *Training*

Step #1: List some of the words that come to mind when you think about "training." Place the words in the chart below.

Step #2: Name the opposite of the words you've listed in Step One. Looking at both sides of any topic (i.e., true/false, positive/negative, right/wrong) can help us come to know a topic more fully.

Step #1 Example: *easy*	Step #2 Example: *hard*

Step #3: Write two sentences about training using two pair of the opposing words from above. For example: *Some days training is* easy *because I feel strong; other days training is* difficult, *and I feel like I'm going backwards and getting weaker.*

Making Meaning Activity: *Training* (cont.)

Step #4: Write a 5-sentence paragraph about <u>training</u> using the guidelines below. This exercise will help you find your "truth" about training.

Sentence 1	a five-word statement
Sentence 2	a question
Sentence 3	two independent clauses combined by a semi-colon
Sentence 4	a sentence with an introductory phrase
Sentence 5	a two-word statement

Quick Response

Write a quick response and a reason why for each:

My favorite training food is . . .

In soccer I am nervous about . . .

My favorite exercise or activity during a training session is . . .

When our team wins a competition by a wide margin, I . . .

When my coach says _____ I feel like . . .

Photo Story

Use your imagination and tell the story of these four soccer players. (If you'd like to know the real story behind the photo, see page 2 of *Writing on the Bus.*)

Injury or Illness

Let's say that you just sprained an ankle. What's the first thing you do? Who do you speak with? Think and write about how you organize yourself to get through an injury or illness.

Proudest Moment

Other than winning a match, tell the story of your proudest moment as a soccer player.

Photo Thoughts

In the space below paste a picture of yourself from a game or training session. The photo could be from a newspaper clipping or Facebook.

Write about what you see, feel, or think when you look at this photograph.

T-shirt Slogans

Come up with four t-shirt slogans/sayings about your team, soccer, competing, or training. Use the t-shirts provided. To jumpstart your thinking, here is the Republic of Ireland's slogan for UEFA Euro 2012:

Talk with your feet. Play with your heart.

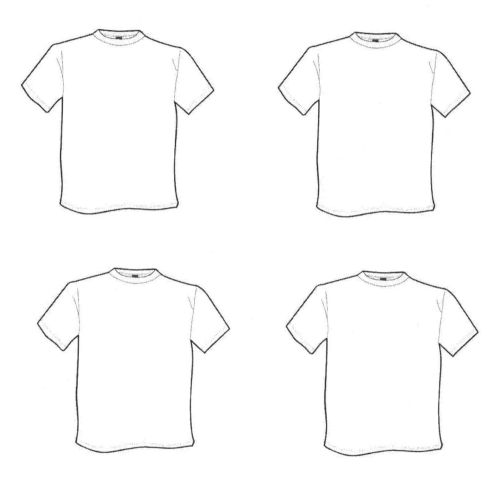

"Do or do not. There is no try."
–Yoda

What might these words from Jedi Master Yoda of Star Wars have to do with playing soccer?

Failure

A class of sports psychology students explored how failure can be helpful. Among the list compiled by students were following—write about them:

Failure found what didn't work.

Failure adds value to success.

Failure creates hunger to do better.

Failure is feedback.

Michael Jordan on Success

Write about this quotation from basketball legend Michael Jordan:

"I've missed more than 9000 shots in my career. I've lost almost 300 games. 26 times, I've been trusted to take the game winning shot and missed. I've failed over and over and over again in my life. And that is why I succeed."

Park Your Feelings

Many times life issues (school, family, relationships, etc.) can impact your ability to focus on soccer during training or a game. To be your best you need to put these distracting thoughts or feelings on the sidelines. Write about a time you had an issue that you brought to the field. Now go back to that game or training session in your head and develop a plan to "park" those feelings or thoughts.

World-Class Thoughts

The following are themes written about in the journal of an elite, world-class athlete:

Loneliness	Relaxation	Lists
Training	Breathing	Equipment
Family	Preparation	Sponsors
Friends	Control	Balance
Focus	Routine	Alignment
Emotions	Yoga	Symmetry
Food	Writing	Asserting
Dreams	Need for	oneself
Body Tension	success	Satisfaction
Colors	Self-esteem	Optimism
Visualization	Playfulness	Goals
Awareness	Schedules	

First, what comes to mind when you read this list?

Second, select one of the themes. Write about the theme for 2-3 minutes and how it relates to you as an athlete.

Performance Analysis

There are times just before a match that you feel "on." You're ready to have at it and everything is in sync. Some days... not so much. Why is that? What specific things affect your performance? Could it be friends, sleep, food, the opponent, your coach, your mood, or even the wrong socks? Make two lists—the good and the bad—of what may influence your performances in a match or training session.

Good Performance *Sample: I know my opponent.*	Bad Performance *Sample: I lack confidence*

Write one or two sentences that capture your thinking about the lists above:

When you were young...

When you were young, whom did you admire as a player and why?

Writing a Match

In this entry you will tell "the story" of one of your games.

Match vs. _____ Date: _____

Describe the evening before this match and discuss whether you prepared (e.g., rested) the way you should have.

How much sleep did you get the night before this match? Is this an optimal amount of sleep for you? What's your goal for sleep the night before a game?

On match day, how did you spend your time? What did you eat? Did you hydrate well? Did you exert energy unnecessarily? If you could improve upon one aspect of preparation for the match, what would that be?

Writing a Match (cont.)

Figure 1 below suggests ways that some players learn about their opponents. On the figure, circle the ways you learned about your opponent for this match. If you have other ways, add them to the figure.

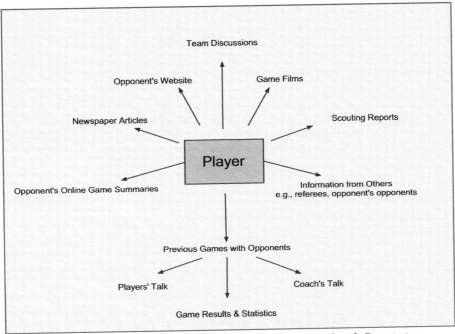

Figure 1, Ways Athletes Learn About an Opponent, Reprinted with Permission

Describe your pre-match "self talk." Were you confident or unsure? Did you visualize your match play?

Writing a Match (cont.)

Describe your pre-game preparation (e.g., warm-up). What one aspect of your warm-ups would you improve upon?

Describe your awareness on the pitch during the match. Did anything take your concentration away from the match? For example, did the opponents' fans draw your attention away from play or did you let other influences (e.g., an official's call, a coach's decision) trouble you?

Describe your post-game recovery (e.g., cool down). Did you stretch, hydrate, and eat appropriately? What one aspect of your post-game recovery would you improve upon?

Sum up your match in a six-word "story." Here's an example: "Yearlong training; offseason camps: Hat Trick!"

Letter to a Former Coach

Write a letter to one of your former coaches. You may wish to include some of the following: what you're doing now as an athlete; this coach's contributions to your athletic and personal life; the issues you currently face as an athlete; a fun memory; and a photo.

Instructional Soccer Video

Think about one of the areas in soccer that you'd like to improve upon like a skill (e.g., heading) or a tactic (e.g., moving to space). Find an instructional video on that topic to watch. You will be able to find many soccer videos on Websites like YouTube. Respond to the following prompts:

Title of Video: _____

Where did you find it: _____

~Discuss the new information you learned from watching this video:

~What might you try out from this video:

~What questions did you have after watching the video:

~What ideas might you share with a teammate or friend:

~What knowledge might you share with your coach:

~What suggestions might you make for revising this video:

A Letter to a Teammate

Write a letter to a teammate, past or present.

The Advantages of Playing Poorly

Why can this statement be true: "Some days, playing poorly is the most important result that could happen." Give examples from your own experiences as a soccer player.

Favorite Sports Movie

What's your favorite sports movie of all time and why? What do you like about the movie? Do you relate to any of the characters? Would you recommend this movie to a younger athlete? If so, why?

"It is more important to participate than to win."

—The Olympic Credo

Write about the Olympic Credo. Why do you think the Olympic Committee adopted this philosophy? Can you give any examples from your own athletic career when you witnessed or experienced this belief in action?

Note to an Opponent

After a game or competition, write a note to an opponent. Highlight the player's strengths or weaknesses, and feel free to offer some advice. Here's an example from a match:

Dear # 3 Right Back,

We played against each other on Thursday night and <u>you could not stop me</u>. Every time I attacked with the ball down the left touchline you lunged at the ball—you ALWAYS tried to take the ball away from me and never tried to delay my attack. My coach tells us that there are four D's in defending—

    -Deny the opponent the ball

    -Delay the opponent when he has the ball

    -Destroy—win the ball!

    -Develop an attack once you have ball

You should practice shadowing an attacking offender, pushing her to the touchline so she can't get a full look at the goal. Delaying stops her from advancing toward the goal and gets other players behind the ball to defend. When the player miskicks the ball or plays it too far ahead, you win the ball. I'm glad I'm not really giving you this letter because I like playing against you! I scored and got two assists. HA! See you in a few weeks, #3!

Your happy opponent,
Stacy
Sailors #9

Space to write your letter is provided on the next page.

Note to an Opponent

Quick Response

Write about the following topics:

Mental preparedness for a match

Coping with Anxiety or Nervousness

Motivation

Managing Success

Handling a loss

How Do You Learn?

How do you learn your sport? Look at this figure and circle the ways you learn as an athlete.

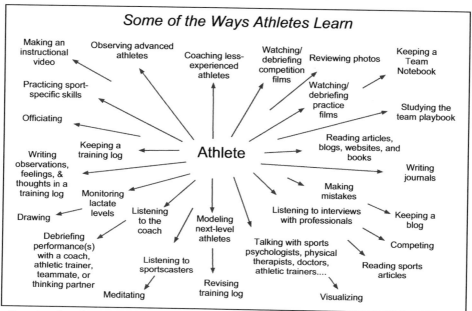

Reprinted with permission, *Writing on the Bus* (Kent, 2012, p. 14)

Looking at the various learning activities above, what could you add to your own experience to help you improve as an athlete?

Are there ways you learn that are not included in the figure above? List them below.

Are you getting enough sleep?

"Sleep is food for the brain."
–The National Sleep Foundation

Go back through your past week and add up the total hours of sleep you've had. Divide the total hours of sleep by the number of days you kept track.

___Total Hours of Sleep ÷ ___ Number of Days = ___ Average Nightly Hours

The National Sleep Foundation suggests that the average teenager needs 9 ¼ hours of sleep per night and the average child aged five to 12 need 10-11 hours of sleep. Add an athlete's lifestyle to the equation and the hours of sleep necessary go up.

–Write about your sleeping habits, especially during the soccer season:

Your Most Humiliating Day as an Athlete

Swedish soccer player Jonathan Szeps wrote the following journal entry as a 17-year old high school exchange student in America:

I easily remember the most humiliating day as an athlete. It was about three years ago when my team had an away game in a suburb called Rinkeby. Rinkeby is one of the suburbs in Sweden with a lot of crime and problems. It is also a suburb with a majority of immigrants. In my team, almost everybody has their roots in Sweden (I'm one of the few who doesn't). Everybody on the team also comes from pretty wealthy families. A lot of my teammates has a lot toward prejudice of Rinkeby. Before the game everybody was joking about how we would get robbed after the game after we easily had defeated the team.

When we arrived to the field the win seemed even more obvious. The field was a joke. Not as big as it should have been in our age, not grass, no nets in the goal and the team we were playing didn't even wear the same uniforms. We expected an easy victory but we were SO WRONG!

The team, called Benadir, gave us a lesson how to play soccer. On a shitty field in the middle of nowhere they played like the Brazilian national team. They played with us, making cool tricks and scoring beautiful goals. At the end of the first half the score was 10-0 and we couldn't believe what we just had experienced. After some yelling from our coach we got back out for second half. We played a little bit better, scoring two goals (I scored one) but we still got beat by 16-2. After the game, instead of robbing us, the players were really nice to us and behaved like a winner should. We were so embarrassed and all of us didn't say a word on way back home. This really proved us wrong about prejudices. I will never forget that loss.

What are your thoughts about Jonathan's experience? Have you had a similar experience in or out of soccer?

Stressed?

The American College of Sports Medicine listed the following signs and symptoms of stress in athletes.

Behavioral	Physical	Psychological
Difficulty sleeping	Feeling ill	Negative self-talk
Lack of focus, overwhelmed	Cold, clammy hands	Inability to concentrate
Consistently performs better in practice/training than in competition	Profuse sweating	Uncontrollable intrusive and negative thoughts or images
Substance abuse	Headaches	Self doubt
	Increased muscle tension	
	Altered appetite	

Referring to the chart above, write about your stress levels in each of the following areas:

Behavioral:

Physical:

Psychological:

Halftime Talk

Using a recent match, make up the halftime talk that you would have given as the opponent's coach. Remember to include as many specifics as possible.

Your Choice

Select one or more of the terms on the left and write:

Poor sport

Great eye

A good loss

Future star

Miscommunication

Injury

Suck-up

Cheat

Focus

Training

Fitness

Teammate

Official

Coach

Trainer

Foul

Frightened

Technical

Discipline

Reward

Practice

Letter to the Opposing Coach

Write a letter to an opposing coach. Here's an example:

Dear Coach,

You have a great team. They are disciplined and organized and the kids were good guys even though they kicked our butts! Your players had wicked good talk. They supported each other with talk. Our coach always tells us to play the way we are facing. At tonight's match I could see that. I was impressed how your midfielders used their defenders so well. They got out of a lot of trouble with quick back passes. I also thought your one and two touch passes were <u>useful</u> as our coach says. We learned a lot today and I am proud of the way we played even though we lost 3-1. Some day I hope our team will play like yours. Good luck with the rest of your season.

Sincerely,

Kevin
#11 Falcon Soccer

Word Clouds

Go back through your journal entries or the *Match Analysis I* that you've completed. Select individual words that reflect you and your season thus far. Using a free online Word Cloud program like Wordle (www.wordle.net) or Tagxedo (www.tagxedo.com), create a word-art interpretation of your sports season so far. Print the Word Cloud, trim it with scissors, and tape it over the model supplied below. If you don't have access to Internet, sketch your own Word Cloud.

Mental Imagery: Creating Personal and Team Highlight Reels

Think back and recall your best moments as a player. Remember the details of that perfect pass, brilliant header, or powerful run forward that helped produce a goal. Perhaps you shut down the other team's leading scorer. Now, make a list of those moments and create your own mental video that you can play back to yourself to prepare for a game or use during a match to gain back confidence.

Instant Highlight Reel (10 to 30 seconds – all you as a player):

Do the same but include team moments such as stringing a dozen passes together that end in a goal or an overtime win against a higher-seeded team.

Highlight Reel (2 to 5 minutes – personal and as a team):

Songs of My Sport

Make a list of your favorite songs:

Which favorite songs would you play...

The night before an important match:
Song title: _____

Training:
Song title: _____

The morning of a match:
Song title: _____

During a match:
Song title: _____

After an upset win:
Song title: _____

After a loss to an opponent you could have beaten:
Song title: _____

When the season ends:
Song title: _____

Others times: _____
Song title: _____

Others times: _____
Song title: _____

Your Thoughtful Side

Tell about the kindest thing you have ever done as an athlete.

Equipment

Draw a picture of your favorite piece of soccer equipment. Write a title and a caption for your drawing.

Title _____

(drawing box)

Caption _____

_____

Good Words

What special story would you like told about a teammate, coach, fan, or opponent and why?

The Benefits of Journal Writing

Dr. Stephanie Dowrick identifies the following benefits of journaling:

- reduces stress and anxiety
- increases self-awareness
- sharpens mental skills
- promotes genuine psychological insight
- advances creative inspiration and insight
- strengthens coping abilities

As an athlete who has been keeping a team notebook, have you experienced any of these benefits? Explain.

Slow Down the Game

The game of soccer is fast paced and has many decisions. A soccer player's head can be full of clutter (e.g., information from other players, from a coach, fan noise). To slow down the game, refocus, and manage anxiety, many athletes use centering breaths.

Centering Breaths:

- Take a deep breath from your abdomen and feel your neck and shoulder muscles relax as you inhale.
- Inhale for about 6 seconds and exhale slowly for about 8-10 seconds.

Activity:

Write about a time in a game that your head was full of clutter or you were anxious. Go back to that time in your mind and practice using the centering breaths to slow down the game and release the clutter so you can make quicker and spot on decisions.

As you exhale slowly, start to focus on a positive aspect of your play. Keep it simple and use your visual senses to bring this positive picture to life.

For the Love of the Game

Write about this quotation from soccer legend Mia Hamm:

> "Somewhere behind the athlete you've become and the hours of practice and the coaches who have pushed you is a little girl who fell in love with the game and never looked back... play for her."

Sports Psychology

All professional teams and some collegiate teams have the support of sport psychologists. Their work involves helping athletes with issues such as

Mental preparedness	Goal setting
Managing Anxiety	Reward strategies
Coping with Success	Visualization
Handling Failure	Motivation

Has writing in this notebook helped you with any of these concerns. If you're not familiar with some of these terms, just do a quick online search.

Moments of the Season

Throughout a soccer season you experience highs and lows, ups and down. Think back through the season and give quick examples of the following:

I laughed...

I cried or got emotional...

I screamed like a wild person...

I got crazy angry...

I sat and stared in disbelief...

I just didn't care...

I wanted to go hide...

I wanted someone to see...

Your Sports Season

Think about your sports season and draw whatever comes to mind.

Write a caption for this photo:

Caption:_____

_____

What memory or story might this photograph bring to mind from your own
soccer playing days?

Additional Journal Prompts

"No one likes skiing with a cluttered mind, so put it on paper and free some space."

—Carter Robinson

1. *The Natural*: If you're a natural athlete, describe what it's like to someone who is not. If you're not a natural athlete, write about what it's like to train with or compete against someone who is. If you are a natural athlete, what's your biggest frustration. If you are not, why has that been a good thing for you?

2. List ten of your favorite all-time quotations by players and coaches. You may find lists of quotations on the Web.

3. Tell about a time when you were genuinely happy for another athlete's poor performance or loss.

4. Describe your greatest disappointment as an athlete thus far in your career. What did you learn from the experience?

5. Who's the oldest soccer player you know. Describe the player. What characteristics of the soccer player do you admire?

6. Describe your earliest memory as a soccer player.

7. If you could relive one moment as a player, what would it be and why would you want to go back?

8. "Champions aren't made in the gyms. Champions are made from something they have deep inside them ~ a desire, a dream, a vision."
                                                              – Muhammad Ali

Write about this quotation from the great heavy weight boxer Muhammad Ali.

9. Tell about a time when you quit.

10. Have you ever been dishonest as an athlete? If so, why? What did you learn from this experience? If you haven't been dishonest or don't want to write about it, have you witnessed dishonesty on the part of another athlete? If so, how did it make you feel?

11. At the present moment what three non-athletic jobs look as if they might give you the same "feeling" that competitive athletics do? Explain your thinking.

12. Where do you see yourself in the next few years as an athlete?

13. What is something you dislike about yourself as an athlete?

14. Think back to a time when an athlete you knew or admired bombed big-time in an event that he or she was favored to win. Describe your feelings.

15. What is your favorite place to compete and why?

16. Write about a frustrating experience you've had as an athlete.

17. When is training an absolute joy?

18. Under what circumstances would you allow a competitor to beat you on purpose.

19. What books would you recommend to a young athlete?

20. Your coach or assistant coach gave you misinformation before a big competition. For example, perhaps they prepped you for a team that would play a 4-4-2 and the team came in with a completely different formation. How do you respond?

21. Write from the perspective of the top athlete in your sport using any of these prompts—

"When I win a competition by a wide margin, I..."
"My worst performance in the past six months made me feel..."
"When other athletes talk about me they say..."
"I am frightened about..."

22. Tape your favorite newspaper article about your season in the Notes section of this workbook. If you or your team didn't make the newspapers, print and include a favorite Facebook or blog post. Write about what has been written.

23. Write about the following quotation by alpine ski racer Carter Robinson: "No one likes skiing with a cluttered mind, so put it on paper and free some space."

24. Create a crossword puzzle of soccer or your team with a free online program like Puzzle-Maker.com

25. Found Poem: Honest... the following activity is fun and helps athletes see a game more clearly by thinking more deeply. Here are the steps toward creating a Found Poem:

-   Find a newspaper article written about you, your team, or another athlete/team that you admire;

-   Read the article and underline words, phrases, or lines that you like or find interesting. Put those words, phrases, or lines into a non-rhyming poem that tells a story. Here are the opening two paragraphs from an article by Bruce Farrin (*Rumford Times*, 1995) about a regional playoff match. We've highlighted some favorite words and phrases that might be used in a poem. We've added a few of our own words to a Found Poem:

Falcons Advance with Thrilling OT Win

RUMFORD — Just 2:27 into the first overtime, Dusty Hackett scored off a corner kick by Kevin New to give Mountain Valley a come-from-behind 3-2 victory over Gray-New Gloucester in Western B boy' soccer semifinals last Wednesday.

"This game showed that we're an older and more mature team. We kept our composure," said Falcon coach Rich Kent.

Here's the opening to a Found Poem:

OT

New to Hackett
Moves us to the finals.
With composure and maturity
The Falcons nail a come-from-behind
Victory

26. If I were not competing in my sport, I would be _____ because _____. Explain.

27. *What was I thinking?* Go back through your journal and log and pick out the comical, nonsensical, and mindless lines you've written and write them below. Enjoy...

28. Watch a competition on television or online and make a list of the best lines spoken by the commentators, coaches, or athletes.

29. What's your earliest memory of a bitter loss?

27. Video Comments: If you or your team had a video taken of a game, match, race, or performance, write a paragraph summarizing the competition as if you were the team's public relations person or a sports caster summarizing the game for television.

28. If appropriate, trade notebooks with a teammate or friend and write an observation of the athlete with respect to training, competition, or life beyond athletics.

29. Draw a picture of a particular moment from the season.

30. As someone who is keeping a journal, how do you feel about this quotation by Grace Paley: "We write about what we don't know about what we know."

31. Write about this quotation from Boston Marathon winner Amby Burfoot: "To get to the finish line, you'll have to try lots of different paths."

32. Think back to the teams you've been on: what phrase or term was used a lot on each team?

33. Pre-game or pre-competition study: Answer the following about the opponent you are about to face:

> -If you have played this opponent before, what do you
> remember about the last contest?
> -What have reliable sources said about the opponents' strengths/weaknesses?
> -What's one strategy or approach that you or your team should
>   try against this opponent?
> -What's your overall game plan?

34. Write a letter about your training and season to someone who cares about you.

35. What is a good opponent?

36. After a competition you participated in, write a performance analysis of a teammate or fellow athlete.

37. Write some six-word sports stories about your competitions and training. Here's an example from a hockey playoff game: "Into OT— Hail Mary empty netter."

38. Write about an athlete who is a "poser." Why do you think this happens to some athletes? When, if ever, have you come close to being a poser? Why do you think it happened to you?

39. One writing scholar wrote the following:

"Writing organizes and clarifies our thoughts. Writing is how we think our way into a subject and make it our own. Writing enables us to find out what we know—and what we don't know—about whatever we're trying to learn."
–William Zinsser, *Writing to Learn*

In what ways is this quotation true for you as an athlete who keeps a Team Notebook?

40. Why can taking a day off be difficult for you?

41. Look back at the results of the last competition you won or did well in. Think about the losing team or look at the name and time of the last-place finisher. Write from the perspective of a player on the losing team or the last-place finisher.

42. Write a conversation between you and an incredibly gifted young athlete who is not living up to her or his potential.

43. Write about the following quotation by Alberto Tomba, an Italian Ski Racer: "In life, I have but one simple desire: To tear down the sky."

44. What advice or talk do you <u>least</u> like to hear before an important soccer match and why?

45. Describe an athlete you would never want to be a teammate with.

46. Write down the details of an amazing match that you watched.

47. What's the best competition you've ever seen in person as a fan?

48. Remember and write about the biggest disappointment you've experienced as an athlete.

49. Practicing to the Next Level: Write about a recent practice session. What could you have done differently to move toward the next level?

50. Truth is, this season...

Team-Building Activities

Team-Building Activities

During different times of the season, your coach will divide the team into small groups of 2-4 athletes. Each group will discuss and come to an agreement on the responses for the following activities. Some times your group's responses will be shared with the entire team; other times, the discussions and results will remain among the group members. If your coach chooses not to use these activities, you may complete most of these on your own or with teammates as Athletic Journal entries.

Tag a Teammate

Under each category, name a teammate. Give an example or two of the athlete's qualities.

Tag a Teammate

Who'd make a great coach?	A true sportsman	Dedication plus	Kindest
Most coachable	Always leaves it on the field	Most motivating	Great future
Great opponent	Team Leader	Fun	Positive
Healthy	Student-Athlete: the complete package	Who should take the last shot	Fitness Fanatic

Create a *New* Set Piece

Create a new corner kick, free kick, or kick-off to introduce to the team and coaching staff.

So far this season...

The funniest thing we've witnessed...

The happiest we've been...

The thing we thought but did not say to a coach, opponent, official, or teammate...

The moment we wish we could take back...

Why do you play *the beautiful game* of soccer?

All-Time Best Soccer Team

Who would you select to be on the all-time best soccer team in history? Discuss your selection of 11 players and 4 substitutes among your group members and then print your choices on chart paper in team formation. Each group will hang up their chart paper. Staying in your group, go from chart to chart and compare your choices with your teammates' selections. After reviewing all of the charts, feel free to revise your all-time best team with suggestions from those you've seen. Your coaches may end this activity by having you discuss and vote on your team's all-time best soccer team.

Team History

Over the course of several days, seek out as much of your team's history and team trivia as possible. Your group will look for traditional soccer records as well as the unconventional. Here is a small list to jumpstart your group's thinking:

Top Goal Scorer

Top Assist Leader

Top Goalkeeper

Overall team record

Championships

Coaches

Assistants

Goals Scored

All-conference

All-League

All-State players

Most cards

Uniforms photos

What We Think About...

What we think about during training.

What we think about during a match.

What we think about after a win.

What we think about after a loss.

At This Moment...

Write about the following as they pertain to your group at this point in the season.

Training

Matches

Coaching

Rest

Nutrition

Travel to away matches

Life beyond sport (e.g., family, school, work)

The rest of the season

What we need right now

The Season's Stats

Come up with as many statistics as possible from your competitive season thus far. These stats may be serious or not. Many figures will be estimated. Here are a few ideas to jumpstart your list—you may want to use a Notes Pages at the back of your notebook to complete the list:

-How many training hours?

-Number of miles traveled to matches?

-How many matches?

-How many hours/miles run?

-Stats about scores, wins, losses, and draws.

-How many hours lifting weights?

How many bananas eaten?

-How often did you stop at fast-food place after a competition or practice?

More:

_____

_____

_____

_____

_____

_____

This Season

What are you going to miss about this season?

Injury Rehabilitation Plan

Instructions for Injury Rehabilitation Plan

Part of playing soccer can include getting injured. How you manage your rehabilitation has a great deal to do with how quickly you'll be back on the pitch. Sit with your athletic trainer, doctor, or coach and fill out the Injury Rehabilitation Plan. Understanding your plan and staying organized will get you back into the game sooner.

-MODEL-

Injury Rehabilitation Plan

Injury Date: *Tuesday, July 18*   Trainer: *Aaron P.*

Diagnosis: *moderate ankle sprain*

Projected Timeline to Recovery: *7-10 days . . . <u>approximately</u>.*

Rehabilitation Plan:

Tuesday: RICE (Rest, Ice, Compression and Elevation). ACE bandage. Keep elevated. Check with parents about using anti-inflammatory medications for pain relief. Wednesday: keep elevated during school. See me in the afternoon.

Training Plan while Injured:

Wednesday: depending on severity use the weight room and swimming pool. Ice therapy w/ me.
Thursday: RICE, keep elevated in school, see me . . . pool?
Friday: keep elevated, RICE, see me, pool.
Saturday: TBA . . . see me on Friday

What can you do to improve an aspect of your play while rehabilitating?

Swimming for upper body. Watch game videos. Stay connected with teammates.

What can you do for your teammates and coaches while rehabilitating?

> *–Don't whine about the injury.*
> *–Stay positive about recovery.*

Other thoughts:

Stay in the game!

*Adapted from Temple University Lacrosse

Injury Rehabilitation Plan

Injury Date:

Diagnosis:

Projected Timeline to Recovery:

Rehabilitation Plan:

Training Plan while Injured:

What can you do to improve an aspect of your play while rehabilitating?

What can you do for your teammates and coaches while rehabilitating?

Other thoughts:

Injury Rehabilitation Plan

Injury Date:

Diagnosis:

Projected Timeline to Recovery:

Rehabilitation Plan:

Training Plan while Injured:

What can you do to improve an aspect of your play while rehabilitating?

What can you do for your teammates and coaches while rehabilitating?

Other thoughts:

Notes Pages

"We write about what we don't know about what we know."

—Grace Paley

Date_____   Title_____

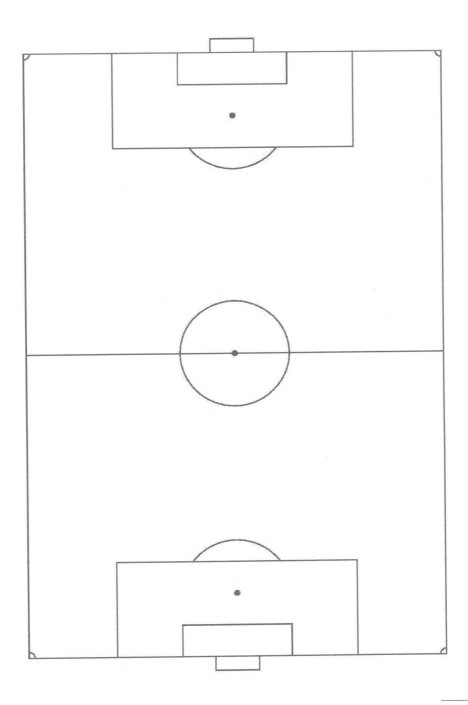

Date_____   Title_____

Notes

Date_____   Title_____

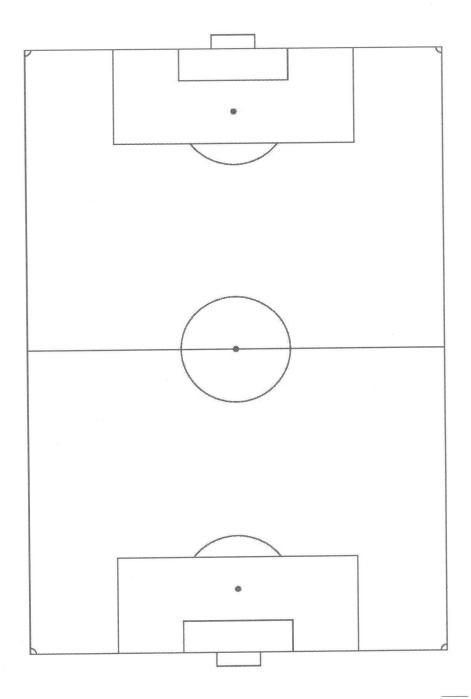

Date_____   Title_____

Notes

Date_____   Title_____

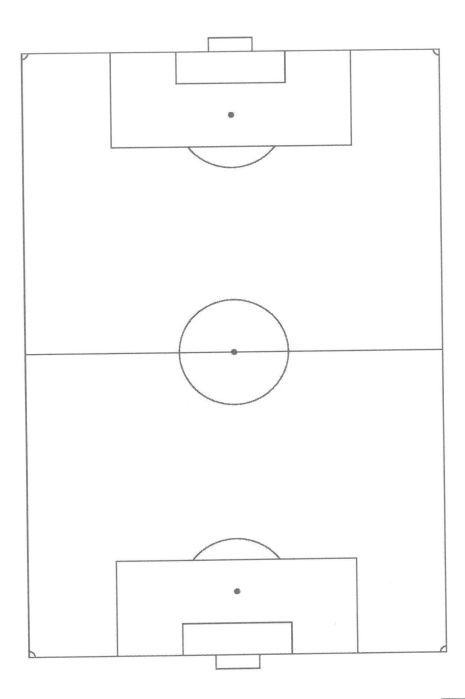

Date_____   Title_____

Notes

Date_____   Title_____

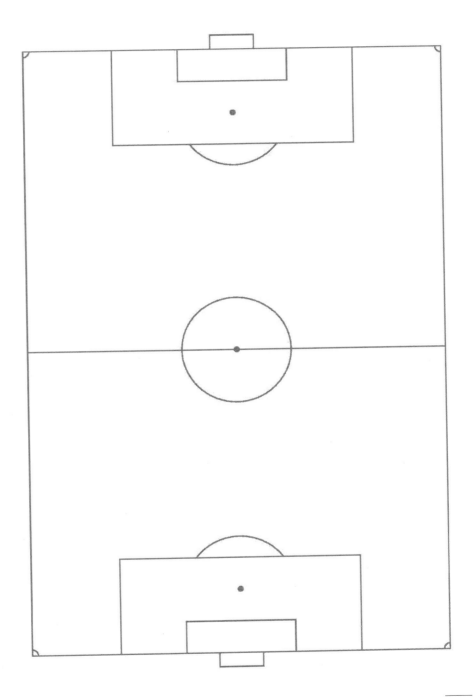

Date_____   Title_____

Notes

Date_____   Title_____

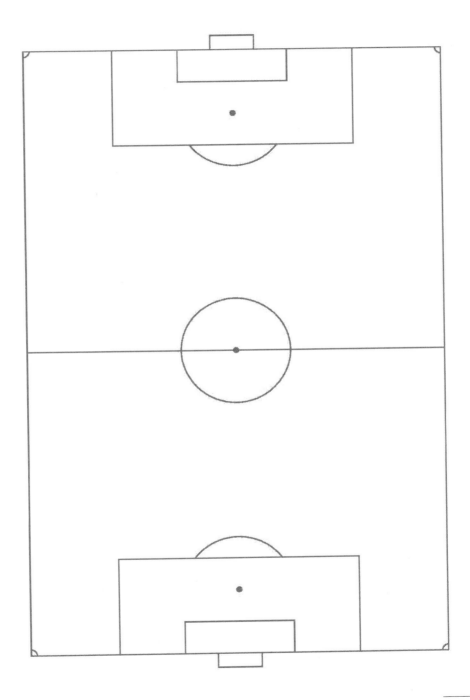

Date_____   Title_____

Notes

Date_____   Title_____

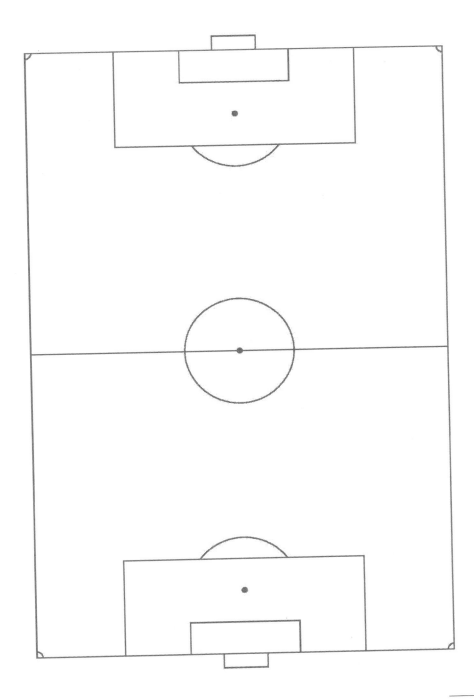

Date_____   Title_____

Notes

Date_____   Title_____

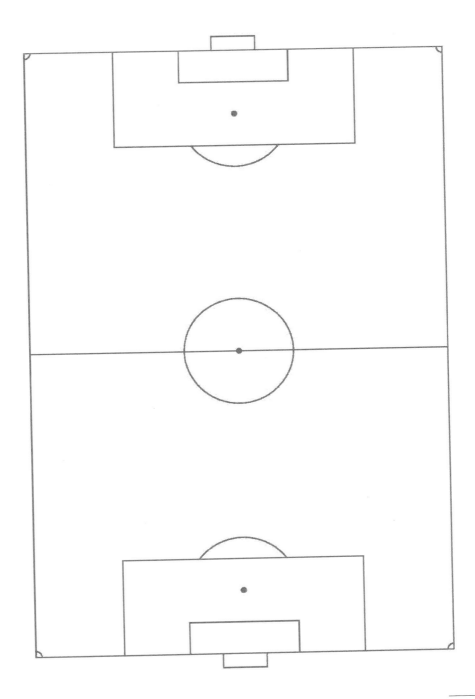

Date_____ Title_____

Notes

Date_____   Title_____

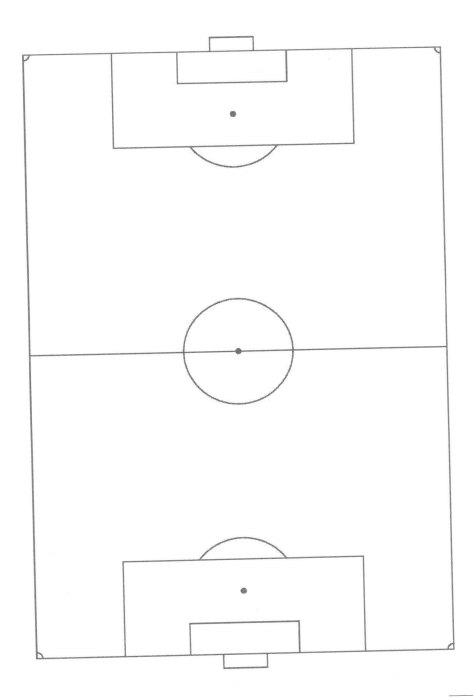

Date_____   Title_____

Notes

Date_____   Title_____

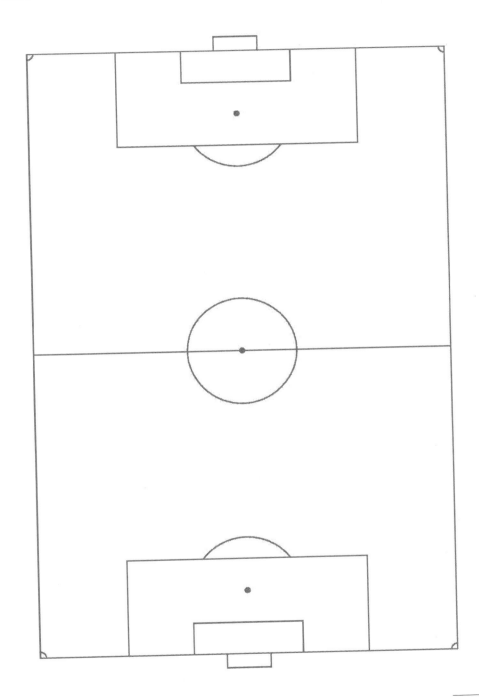

Date_____   Title_____

Notes

Date_____   Title_____

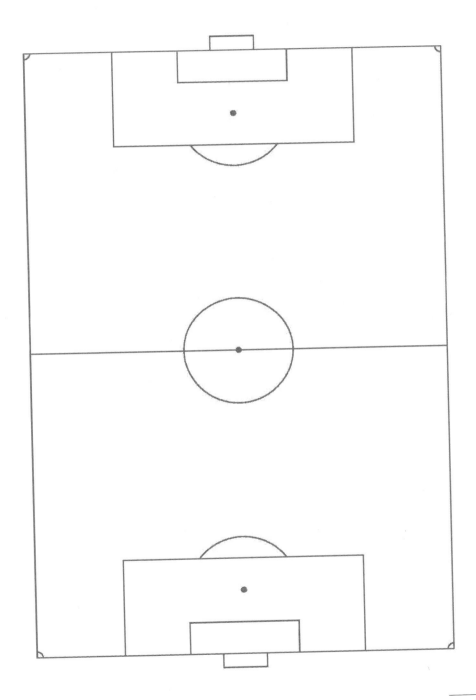

Date_____   Title_____

Notes

Date_____   Title_____

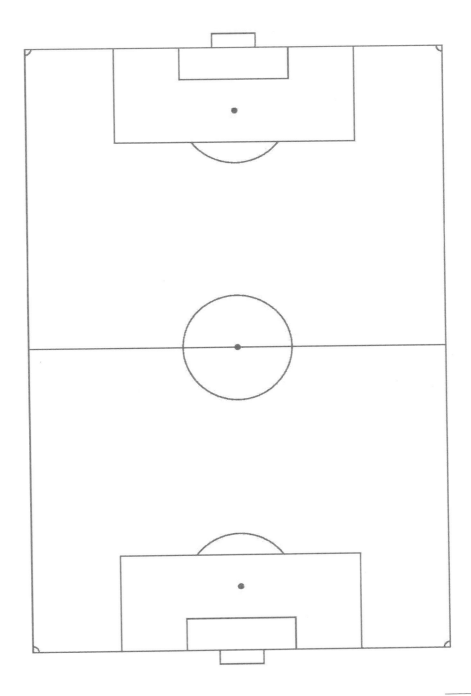

Date_____   Title_____

Notes

Coach's Comments

"A good coach will make ... players see what they can be rather than what they are."

—Ara Parseghian

Coach's Comments   Date_____

Coach's Comments   Date_____

Coach's Comments   Date_____

Authors

Richard Kent

Amy Edwards

Richard Kent is a professor at the University of Maine and the director of the Maine Writing Project, a site of the National Writing Project. He is the author of 10 books, including *Writing on the Bus*, *The Athlete's Workbook*, and *Play On!* In 1979, Kent started high school soccer in his hometown of Rumford, Maine. He brought 30 State of Maine select teams to England over a 13-year period and studied soccer in Brazil.

Amy Edwards is the Head Women's Soccer Coach at Gonzaga University and has been a collegiate coach since 1993. She started her coaching career working in youth clubs and continued in the Olympic Development Programs of Oklahoma and Missouri. Coach Edwards holds national coaching licenses from both USSF and NSCAA.

Write. Learn. Perform.
Play On!